Animals in the W[ild]

Bird of Prey

by Mary Hoffman

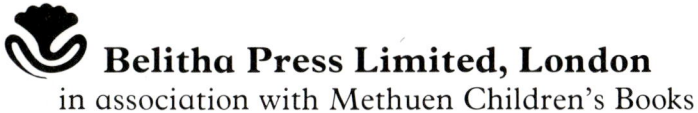

Belitha Press Limited, London
in association with Methuen Children's Books

This kestrel chick is the first to hatch out of its egg. It doesn't look much like a bird of prey yet, but it will have a powerful beak and claws when it grows.

These red kite chicks are birds of prey too.
You can see they already have curved beaks.
A bird of prey eats other birds or mammals.
Some eat fish or snakes or insects.

The osprey is one which eats fish. This osprey is trying to shade her chick from the sun. Birds of prey do their hunting during the day, unlike owls, who hunt at night.

4

In Africa there is an unusual bird of prey called the secretary-bird. One parent guards the chicks while the other hunts for food. These two secretary-birds are changing over nest duty.

This is a grown-up kestrel with its chicks.
Kestrels usually take over another bird's nest.
But many birds of prey come back to
the same nests every year to lay their eggs.

Eagles build their own nests. This golden eagle has nested on a cliff. It is feeding the chick with meat. The parent bird swallows the food and then regurgitates it for the chick to eat.

This young buzzard is stretching its wings to make them strong. Birds of prey have to be good at flying. They sometimes have to fly a long way to find food.

If you live very high up, like these young prairie falcons in South Dakota, USA, your first flight will be easier. When they are ready to fly, the falcons will launch themselves on to the hot air currents.

When it flies, a bird of prey does not flap its wings much. It spreads its tail and wing feathers and soars through the air.

This is a merlin in full flight.

The bird of prey flies along until it sees something to eat. We don't know what this buzzard has seen, but it is now doing its hunting stoop, with its talons stretched out.

This sea-eagle has its talons ready to grab a fish under the water.

But this eagle is having some trouble getting a heavy fish out of the water.

The martial eagle from Africa has caught a squirrel. You can see how well its beak and talons are suited to this kind of hunting.

Some birds of prey eat snakes. This is a red-tailed hawk, which has caught a rattlesnake. A bird must be very quick to catch a snake.

There is one group of birds of prey that doesn't catch live food. These are the vultures. The gazelle in the picture has died or been killed by another animal. The vultures are coming to eat it.

Dead food is called carrion. Many people think that vultures are disgusting, because they eat carrion. But vultures are very useful – if they didn't eat dead animals, the bodies would go bad.

So vultures stop diseases from spreading by eating the meat before it starts to rot. Vultures do not spend much time waiting in trees like this. They watch other vultures and see where they land.

All the vultures you have seen so far live in Africa. But there are vultures in South America too. This amazing-looking bird is the king vulture. When he arrives, all the other vultures let him eat first.

The secretary-bird has very long legs, which make it the tallest bird of prey.

The smallest bird of prey also lives in Africa. It is a pygmy falcon. It is only 15 cm long but it can kill smaller birds as well as insects.

In general, birds of prey do not disturb animals which they can't eat. This Galapagos hawk is using the giant tortoise as a landing-platform. It couldn't turn the tortoise over or eat it.

For hundreds of years, people have trained some kinds of birds of prey to hunt for them. This falconer is talking to his peregrine falcon. These birds have a very close relationship with humans.

Index

buzzard	8, 11
chicks	2-7, 9
eagle	title page, 7, 12-14, back cover
food	3, 7, 11-17
goshawk	front cover
kestrel	2, 6
merlin	10
nests	5-7
osprey	4
peregrine falcon	23
prairie falcon	9
red kite	3
red-tailed hawk	15
secretary-bird	5, 20
vulture	16-19

Useful words about birds of prey

carrion	dead animals eaten by vultures and other creatures
chick	a baby bird
diurnal	by day. A bird of prey is a diurnal hunter
prey	animals which are killed for food
raptor	another word for a bird of prey. It means a snatcher!
regurgitate	bring back food previously swallowed
stoop	the hunting dive of a bird of prey
talons	big curved claws

First published 1987 by Belitha Press Limited, 31 Newington Green, London N16 9PU in association with Methuen Children's Books Ltd, 11 New Fetter Lane, London EC4 4EE
Text and illustrations in this format copyright © Belitha Press 1987
Text copyright © Mary Hoffman 1987
Scientific Adviser: Dr Gwynne Vevers. Picture Researcher: Stella Martin. Design: Ken Hatherley
Acknowledgements are due to the following for the photographs used in this book: Bruce Coleman Ltd pp. 2, 3, 7, 8, 10, 12, 13, 17, 18, 19, 20, 21, 23 and back cover; Oxford Scientific Films Ltd pp. 1 and 9; Survival Anglia Ltd pp. 4 and 11; Natural Science Photos p. 5; NHPA pp. 6 and 14; Frank Lane Picture Agency pp. 15, 16, 22 and front cover.
All rights reserved. No part of this publication may be reproduced, stored in a retrieval system, or transmitted, in any form or by any means, electronic, mechanical, photocopying, recording or otherwise, without the prior permission of the publishers.
ISBN 0 416 01732 0   Printed in Hong Kong by South China Printing Co.

Dedicated to Stevie